LOW CARB
CHICKEN
SLOW COOKER
COOKBOOK

40 Easy Delicious Low Carb
Slow Cooker Chicken Recipes
for Extreme Weight Loss

Disclaimer

The information in this book is not to be used as medical advice. The recipes should be used in combination with guidance from your physician. Please consult your physician before beginning any diet. It is especially important for those with diabetes, and those on medications to consult with their physician before making changes to their diet.

Disclaimer and Terms of Use: Effort has been made to ensure that the information in this book is accurate and complete, however, the author and the publisher do not warrant the accuracy of the information, text and graphics contained within the book due to the rapidly changing nature of science, research, known and unknown facts and internet. The Author and the publisher do not hold any responsibility for errors, omissions or contrary interpretation of the subject matter herein. This book is presented solely for motivational and informational purposes only.

Introduction

Elevate your dining experience with forty low carb chicken slow cooker recipes, each with its own dynamic flavour and incredible herbs and spices. Chicken is an essential component of any dietary program, and it brings essential vitamins, minerals and protein to the low carbohydrate plan.

Reap the rewards of the low carbohydrate lifestyle. Research shows that a low carbohydrate diet is the number one way to lose weight quickly. When you eat carbohydrates, your body converts those carbohydrates to glucose. Glucose is, essentially, a sugar your cells utilize in order to fuel you and allow you to breathe, grow, and think. When you eat low carbohydrate meals, however, your body doesn't have that automatic flux of glucose in its system. It must, instead, transfer the proteins you give it into glucose through several extra steps in the liver. This, in turn, burns extra calories. Your body must further transfer fat into ketones, which is far more beneficial for the kidneys, some parts of the brain, and the heart than the common glucose molecule. Furthermore, your body looks to stored fat in the body to fuel itself, thus allowing you to drop weight. Scientifically speaking, there's no better way to drop weight than with the low carbohydrate lifestyle.

Combining the low carbohydrate diet with chicken, one of the most nutritional foods on the planet, is essential in order to rev your metabolism. Chicken is a white meat that takes on several different flavours in the slow cooker. Create cheese-y Parmesan soup, white chili, rotisserie chicken, and even some low-carb quesadillas, and reap the incredible benefits of the chicken. Chicken is pulsing with tryptophan, an incredible amino acid that lends a comfort, a feeling of solace to you. Furthermore, it boosts your brain's serotonin levels, which works to increase the quality of your sleep, decrease your stress levels, and make you feel more cheerful! Therefore, it elevates the quality of your life. Furthermore, chicken suppresses the amino acid homocysteine, an element that causes cardiovascular disease. As the chicken decreases your stress levels and keeps homocysteine at bay, your interior ticker can continue working its magic for a long, long time.

Chicken, of course, packs a serious protein punch, which, as aforementioned, seriously contributes to your weight loss on a low carb diet as your body transfers it to glucose in the liver. Chicken is further packed with selenium, a mineral that boosts your body's metabolic performance. Therefore, it elevates the functionality of your metabolism, your hormones, and your thyroid gland, which works to help you lose weight. Chicken's great vitamin B count elevates the metabolic cellular reactions in your cells, as well, which works to keep your metabolism eating up the calories you send into your body. This helps your body maintain a steady weight. One of these B vitamins, niacin, works to refute cancer growth in your cells, as well.

Super-charge your health and create flavourful, nutritive recipes with the following forty slow cooker low carbohydrate outlines. Calm yourself, lose weight, and amaze friends and family with the incredible recipes you create!

Table of Contents

WARM WINTER
CHICKEN SOUP
RECIPES

Perfect Parm Chicken Soup

Recipe Makes 4 Servings
**Nutritional Breakdown Per Serving: 210 calories,
4 grams net carbohydrates, 13 grams fat, 17
grams protein**
Prep Time: 10 minutes
Cook Time: 6 hours

Ingredients:
5 cups chicken broth
½ tsp. salt
1 cup water
1 cup diced zucchini
2 diced onions
¼ cup chopped parsley
½ tsp. poultry seasoning
¼ tsp. nutmeg
1/3 cup grated Parmesan cheese
2 diced skinless and boneless chicken breasts
1 tsp. Bouillon beef

Directions:
Begin by preparing the vegetables and dicing the
chicken. Place the chicken broth, salt, water, zucchini,
onions, parsley, poultry seasoning, and the beef
bouillon in the slow cooker. Cover the slow cooker
and cook on LOW for five hours. Afterwards, add the
nutmeg and the chicken and cook for an additional

hour. Pour in the grated Parmesan cheese and allow it to melt. Salt and pepper to taste, if you please, and enjoy with salt and pepper.

Veggie Chicken Soup

Recipe Makes 9 Servings
Nutritional Breakdown Per Serving: 100 calories, 6 grams net carbohydrates, 4 grams fat, 9 grams protein
Prep Time: 10 minutes
Cook Time: 7 hours

Ingredients:

1 diced onion

5 minced garlic cloves

1 chopped celery stalk

1 tbsp. paprika

1 diced carrot

1 bay leaf

1 tsp. cinnamon

3 tsp. turmeric

15 ounces diced tomatoes

1 ½ cups spinach

10 ounces green beans

4 cups chicken broth

1 tbsp. olive oil

2 diced chicken breasts

Directions:

Begin by preparing the vegetables and dicing the chicken. To the side, pour the olive oil into a skillet and cook the onions, garlic, and the celery together for about seven minutes. Add this mixture to the slow cooker. Bring everything else into the slow cooker, as well, and place the lid on the slow cooker. Allow the soup to cook for seven hours on LOW and enjoy warm.

Spiced Chicken Soup

Recipe Makes 8 Servings
Nutritional Breakdown Per Serving: 220 calories, 9 grams net carbohydrates, 13 grams fat, 17 grams protein
Prep Time: 10 minutes
Cook time: 5 hours

Ingredients:
5 cups water
2 diced chicken breasts
½ shredded cabbage
1 diced onion
8 ounces green chilies
15 ounces diced tomatoes
1 tbsp. garlic salt
4 tbsp. heavy whipping cream
8 ounces softened cream cheese

1 ½ cups salsa
1 tbsp. cumin
salt and pepper to taste

Directions:

Begin by placing the diced chicken, cabbage, and the onion in the slow cooker. Pour over the water. Cook this on high for four hours. Afterwards, add everything else: chilies, tomatoes, whipping cream, cream cheese, salsa, and the spices. Stir well. Cook for an additional thirty minutes and enjoy warm.

Greek Avgolemono Chicken Soup

Recipe Makes 8 Servings
Nutritional Breakdown Per Serving: 123 calories, 8 grams net carbohydrates, 4 grams fat, 14 grams protein
Prep Time: 45 minutes
Cook Time: 4 hours

Ingredients:
5 cups shredded chicken
9 cups chicken broth
3 eggs
½ cup lemon juice
2 cups spaghetti squash
1/3 cup chopped parsley
salt and pepper to taste

Directions:

Begin by making the spaghetti squash. Halve a spaghetti squash and place it face down in the oven. Bake for forty minutes. Afterwards, remove the spaghetti squash and parse at it with a fork to create your "spaghetti."

Next, pour the chicken and the broth into the slow cooker. Cook these ingredients together on HIGH for three minutes. After three hours, whisk together the lemon juice and the eggs and pour this mixture into the slow cooker. Add the spaghetti squash and cook for an additional thirty minutes on LOW. Salt and pepper the soup to taste, and enjoy.

Paleo Fajita Soup

Recipe Makes 8 Servings
Nutritional Breakdown Per Serving: 245 calories,
3 grams net carbohydrates, 18 grams fat, 21
grams protein
Prep Time: 10 minutes
Cook Time: 6 hours

Ingredients:
2 pounds diced chicken breasts
4 cups chicken stock
15 ounces diced tomatoes
4 minced garlic cloves
4 ounces green chilies
10 ounces enchilada sauce
½ tsp. salt
1/8 tsp. pepper
1 ½ tsp. paprika
1 tbsp. chili powder
1 diced jalapeno
1 diced red pepper
½ tsp. cayenne
1 tsp. oregano
juice from 2 limes
¼ cup cilantro

Directions:

Begin by slicing and dicing the vegetables and the chicken breasts. Bring everything into the slow cooker except the cilantro and the lime juice. Stir for a moment and put the lid back on the slow cooker.

Cook the mixture on LOW for six hours. Afterwards, stir in the cilantro and the lime juice, serve warm.

Autumn Pumpkin and Chicken Chowder

Recipe Makes 16 Servings
Nutritional Breakdown Per Serving: 150 calories, 10 grams net carbohydrates, 8 grams fat, 11 grams protein
Prep Time: 15 minutes
Cook Time: 8 hours

Ingredients:
2 diced red peppers
2 diced jalapeno peppers
1 ½ pounds diced skinless and boneless chicken breasts
3 diced leeks
1 diced pumpkin
1 tsp. chili powder
1 tsp. salt
1 cup corn
3 tbsp. almond flour
15 ounces chicken broth
1 tbsp. oregano
½ cup sour cream
2 tbsp. olive oil

Directions:
Begin by pouring the olive oil into a skillet and frying up the peppers for about five minutes. Afterwards,

pour the peppers and the oil into the slow cooker. Add the rest of the prepared ingredients—except for the sour cream—to the slow cooker, and cover the slow cooker. Allow the soup to cook on LOW for seven hours. After seven hours, add the sour cream and stir well. Allow the soup to cook for an additional thirty minutes with the cover off. Serve warm.

Paleolithic Diet Chicken Tortilla Soup

Recipe Makes 6 Servings
Nutritional Breakdown Per Serving: 215 calories, 4 grams net carbohydrates, 12 grams fat, 13 grams protein
Prep Time: 15 minutes
Cook Time: 3 hours

Ingredients:

2 diced chicken breasts
28 ounces diced tomatoes
28 ounces chicken broth
2 diced onions
2 cups diced carrots
2 diced jalapenos
5 minced garlic cloves
1 tsp. cumin
2 tbsp. tomato paste
1 tbsp. olive oil
2 cups diced celery
1 tsp. chili powder

Directions:

Begin by pouring the bit of olive oil into the slow cooker and adding ¼ cup of chicken broth. Afterwards, toss in the prepared onions, jalapenos, garlic, salt, and pepper. Allow them to cook together on HIGH heat for just a few minutes.

Afterwards, add the rest of the ingredients and water to completely fill the pot. Cover the slow cooker and allow the soup to cook for two hours.

After the chicken is cooked, shred it with two forks while it's still in the slow cooker. Stir the soup well and enjoy.

Stormy Weather Low Carb Tomato and Chicken Soup

Recipe Makes 24 Servings
Nutritional Breakdown Per Serving: 200 calories, 4 grams net carbohydrates, 10 grams fat, 20 grams protein
Prep Time: 10 minutes
Cook Time: 6 hours

Ingredients:
2 - 3 pound chickens
3 tbsp. olive oil
4 diced leeks
500 ml chicken broth
½ cup white wine
5 minced garlic cloves
4 tbsp. chopped parsley
½ tsp. cinnamon

2 cups diced tomatoes

1 tsp. chili flakes

1/3 cup cream

5 tbsp. vegetable oil

1 tsp. ginger

Directions:

Begin by slicing up the chicken. Pour the olive oil into the slow cooker, and place the chicken pieces on top. Next, add the rest of the ingredients to the slow cooker. Stir well, and place the lid over the chicken. Allow the soup to cook on LOW for six hours. Enjoy.

AUTUMN
CHICKEN CHILI
RECIPES

Pumpkin Chicken Chili

Recipe Makes 8 Servings
Nutritional Breakdown Per Serving: 290 calories,
4 grams net carbohydrates, 20 grams fat, 22
grams protein
Prep Time: 10 minutes
Cook Time: 6 hours

Ingredients:
5 cups chicken broth
2 cups diced pumpkin
4 cups shredded and cooked chicken
1 tbsp. diced chipotle peppers
1 ½ cups chickpeas
1 tsp. coriander
½ cup salsa
3 tsp. cumin

Directions:
Begin by dicing up the pumpkin and shredding the cooked chicken. Place everything together in the slow cooker and stir for a few moments. Place the lid on the slow cooker and cook on LOW for six to eight hours prior to serving with your favourite chili topping. Enjoy.

White Winter Chicken Chili

Recipe Makes 6 Servings
Nutritional Breakdown Per Serving: 215 calories,
8 grams net carbohydrates, 14 grams fat, 14
grams protein
Prep Time: 10 minutes
Cook time: 5 hours

Ingredients:
4 halved chicken breasts
2 cups chicken broth
10 ounces diced green chilies
1 diced onion
white chili seasoning mix
1 cup sour cream

Directions:
Begin by placing everything together in the slow cooker except the sour cream. Stir well and place the lid on the slow cooker. Cook for four and a half hours on HIGH. Afterwards, remove the chicken halves and shred them with two forks. Return the chicken to the chili, and add the sour cream. Stir well and cook for an additional ten minutes. Afterwards, serve warm.

Spicy Chicken Chili

Recipe Makes: 4 Servings
**Nutritional Breakdown Per Serving: 390 calories,
9 grams net carbohydrates, 20 grams fat, 38
grams protein**
Prep Time: 10 minutes
Cook Time: 8 hours

Ingredients:
1 tbsp. olive oil
2 diced onions
3 minced garlic cloves
1 ½ pounds skinless and boneless chicken breasts
1 pound diced tomatillos
2 tsp. cumin
juice from 2 limes
4 cups chopped cilantro
2 diced jalapeno chilies

salt and pepper to taste

Directions:

Begin by pouring the olive oil into a skillet and cooking the onions and the garlic for about five minutes. Pour this mixture into the slow cooker. Next, add the skinless and boneless chicken breasts, cumin, tomatillos, chilies, and salt and pepper.

Put the cover on the slow cooker and allow the chili to cook for seven hours on LOW. Afterwards, remove the chicken and tear it with two forks. Deposit the chicken back into the chili, and stir. Place the lid back on the slow cooker and allow it to cook for an additional forty-five minutes. Serve warm.

Buffalo Wild Chicken Chili

Recipe Makes 8 Servings
**Nutritional Breakdown Per Serving: 250 calories,
8 grams net carbohydrates, 12 grams fat, 24
grams protein**
Prep Time: 10 minutes
Cook Time: 8 hours

Ingredients:
1 tbsp. olive oil
1 diced carrot
2 diced onions
2 tbsp. chili powder
5 minced garlic cloves
2 chopped celery stalks
2 pounds ground chicken
2 cups chicken broth
1 tbsp. cumin
1 ½ tbsp. paprika
15 ounces tomato sauce
15 ounces diced tomatoes
salt and pepper to taste

Directions:
Begin by slicing and dicing all the vegetables. Place the olive oil at the bottom of the slow cooker, and add the vegetables. Stir for a moment. Afterwards, add the spices, chicken, and the tomatoes. Pour in the

chicken broth and stir. Place the lid on the slow cooker and allow it to cook for 8 hours on LOW. Enjoy warm.

WARM-UP
CHICKEN STEW
RECIPES

Savoury Chicken Stew

Recipe Makes 6 Servings
Nutritional Breakdown Per Serving: 230 calories,
8 grams net carbohydrates, 14 grams fat, 19
grams protein
Prep Time: 10 minutes
Cook time: 6 hours

Ingredients:
4 cups diced cabbage
1 diced carrot
1 diced onion
3 diced celery stalks
26 ounces diced tomato
14 ounces chicken stock
¼ tsp. pepper
½ tsp. salt
5 skinless and boneless chicken breasts

3 cups spinach

Parmesan cheese

Directions:

Bring all of the ingredients together in the slow cooker except for the spinach and the Parmesan. Stir well, and place the lid on the slow cooker. Cook the stew on HIGH for five hours. Afterwards, remove the chicken and tear it apart with two forks. Return the chicken, and place the spinach into the slow cooker. Keep the lid off the slow cooker and allow it to cook for an additional one hour.

Serve warm with Parmesan cheese on top.

Marvellous Mushroom Chicken Stew

Recipe Makes 10 Servings
Nutritional Breakdown Per Serving: 275 calories,
9.8 gram net carbohydrates, 8 grams fat, 10
grams protein
Prep Time: 15 minutes
Cook time: 9 hours

Ingredients:
15 ounces mushroom soup
2 diced onions
2 minced garlic cloves
1 diced celery stalk
3 cups water
2 cups processed rice-like cauliflower
4 diced chicken breasts

Direction:
Begin by placing the mushroom soup into the slow cooker. Add the four chicken breasts, onion, garlic, pepper, and the celery. Afterwards, stir well and place the lid on the slow cooker. Allow the chicken to cook for eight hours. Afterwards, take the breasts out and tear them apart with two forks.

Right before serving, process the cauliflower into two cups of rice-like material. Pour the cauliflower into the stew, and stir well prior to serving it warm.

Cheese-y Chicken and Garlic Broccoli Stew

Recipe Makes 12 Servings
Nutritional Breakdown Per Serving: 308 calories, 4 grams net carbohydrates, 23 grams fat, 22 grams protein
Prep Time: 10 minutes
Cook Time: 8 hours

Ingredients:

½ cup melted butter
2 diced onions
4 minced garlic cloves
½ pound cubed cheddar cheese
½ pound softened sour cream
14 ounces chicken broth
16 ounces diced broccoli
1 tbsp. garlic powder
2 cups whole milk
1 cup corn starch
1 cup water
3 diced chicken breasts

Directions:

Begin by melting the butter in the skillet, and pour the onions and garlic into the butter. Cook the onion and garlic for about five minutes. Pour this mixture into the slow cooker and add the rest of the ingredients, including the diced chicken. Stir well. Allow the stew to cook for eight hours in the slow cooker. Try to stir the soup every few hours to allow the cheese to assimilate with the rest of the ingredients. Serve warm.

Grumpy Day Garlic Stew

Recipe Makes 6 Servings
Nutritional Breakdown Per Serving: 150 calories, 7 grams net carbohydrates, 10 grams fat, 13 grams protein
Prep Time: 10 minutes
Cook Time: 5 hours

Ingredients:

20 unpeeled garlic cloves
12 peeled garlic cloves
3 tbsp. butter
2 tbsp. olive oil
1 sliced onion
4 cups chicken stock
¾ cup whipping cream
2 pounds cubed chicken thighs
salt and pepper to taste

Directions:

Begin by bringing the butter and olive oil together in a skillet. Add the onion to the skillet and allow it to cook for about five minutes. Pour this mixture into the slow cooker. Next, add the chicken stock, chicken thighs, garlic cloves—both peeled and unpeeled— and the salt and pepper. Place the lid on the slow cooker and allow it to cook on LOW for eight hours. Afterwards, pour this mixture into a blender. Add the cream and blend the ingredients until completed pureed. Return the mixture to the slow cooker and allow it to cook for an additional twenty minutes. Serve warm.

Cilantro Chicken Stew

Recipe Makes 8 Servings
Nutritional Breakdown Per Serving: 130 calories, 6 grams net carbohydrates, 4 grams fat, 14 grams protein
Prep Time: 15 minutes
Cook Time: 8 hours

Ingredients:
1 tbsp. olive oil
5 minced garlic cloves
4 diced onions
1 tsp. cumin
½ diced red pepper
1 tsp. annatto seed powder
4 diced skinless and boneless chicken breasts
1 tsp. garlic powder
4 ounces light beer (it will cook out)

1 cup water
1 cup chopped cilantro

Directions:

Begin by prepping all the ingredients. Pour everything into the slow cooker, including the light beer and the diced chicken breasts. Do not add the cilantro. Stir the stew, and place the lid on the slow cooker. Cook the stew for a full seven hours. Afterwards, stir and add the cilantro. Keep the lid off the slow cooker and allow it to cook for an additional hour. Serve warm.

African Wind Chicken Stew

Recipe Makes 8 Servings
**Nutritional Breakdown Per Serving: 270 calories,
5 grams net carbohydrates, 20 grams fat, 20
grams protein**
Prep Time: 15 minutes
Cook Time: 6 hours

Ingredients:
3 tbsp. olive oil
1 diced onion
1 tbsp. ginger
1 tsp. chili powder
2 tsp. jalapeno chilies
1 cup chicken stock
2 tbsp. tomato paste
1 ½ tbsp. apple cider vinegar
3 cups diced chicken

Directions:
Begin by preparing the various vegetables. Bring
everything into the slow cooker and allow it to cook
on LOW for six hours. Afterwards, top the stew with
your choice of shredded cheese, and salt and pepper
everything. Enjoy!

ALL DAY AWAY
CHICKEN
RECIPES

Western Plain Buffalo Chicken

Recipe Makes 6 Servings
**Nutritional Breakdown Per Serving: 150 calories,
8 grams net carbohydrates, 3 grams fat, 33 grams
protein**
Prep Time: 10 minutes
Cook Time: 4 hours

Ingredients:
2 pounds skinless, boneless chicken
2 celery stalks
2 carrots
1 quartered onion
3 garlic cloves
2 cups chicken broth
2/3 cup low-carb buffalo sauce (I used Frank's)

Directions:
Place the chicken, celery, garlic, onion, carrots, and
the broth into the slow cooker. Salt and pepper the
mixture and place the lid on the slow cooker. Allow
the chicken to cook on HIGH for four hours.
Afterwards, remove about a third of the cooking juice
and all the vegetables.

Shred the chicken in the slow cooker with forks and
add the buffalo sauce. Allow this to cook for an

additional fifteen minutes. Serve warm with the vegetables as a side.

Hellas Feta-Stuffed Chicken

Recipe Makes 6 Servings
Nutritional Breakdown Per Serving: 200 calories, 4 grams net carbohydrates, 5 grams fat, 34 grams protein
Prep Time: 15 minutes
Cook Time: 4 hours

Ingredients:
2 pounds skinless and boneless chicken breasts
3 diced red peppers
4 cups chopped spinach
1 cup diced artichokes
5 ounces feta cheese
¼ cup diced black olives
1 tbsp. chopped oregano
2 cups chicken broth
1 tsp. garlic powder

Directions:

Begin by mixing together the red peppers, feta, artichokes, spinach, garlic, and oregano. Salt and pepper the chicken breasts, and make a pocket in each chicken breast with a sharp knife. Do not cut through the chicken.

Next, stuff each chicken breast with the prepared mixture. Place the chicken in the slow cooker. You might have to seat each chicken "vertically" with the spinach pointing up. Pour the chicken broth over the chicken and allow the chicken to cook on LOW for four hours. Enjoy!

Thai-Smile Curry Chicken

Recipe Makes 8 Servings
Nutritional Breakdown Per Serving: 240 calories, 5 grams net carbohydrates, 10 grams fat, 35 grams protein
Prep Time: 10 minutes
Cook Time: 4 ½ hours

Ingredients:

15 ounces coconut milk

4 tbsp. green curry paste

3 tbsp. brown sugar

2 ½ pounds diced chicken breasts

8 ounces mini corn

1 diced red onion

2 tbsp. water

2 tbsp. cornstarch

4 minced garlic cloves

Directions:

Pour the coconut milk, brown sugar, garlic, and the green curry paste in the slow cooker and stir well. Next, toss in the prepared vegetables and the chicken. Place the lid on the slow cooker and allow the mixture to cook for four hours on LOW.

After four hours, pour in the water and the cornstarch. Stir well, and cook for an additional thirty minutes. Stir occasionally, and serve warm.

What-A-Jerk Chicken

Recipe Makes 12 Servings
Nutritional Breakdown Per Serving: 105 calories, 2 grams net carbohydrates, 2 grams fat, 18 grams protein
Prep Time: 10 minutes
Cook Time: 6 hours

Ingredients:
3 pounds skinless and boneless chicken thighs
juice from 1 lime
5 minced garlic cloves
1 tbsp. ginger
2 tbsp. thyme
2 tsp. allspice berries
1 tsp. salt
2 tbsp. apple cider vinegar
4 sliced chili peppers

4 diced scallions

1 tbsp. brown sugar

1 diced red pepper

Directions:

Begin by placing the chicken in the slow cooker. To the side, add the ingredients into a blender and completely puree them. Pour this mixture over the chicken, and place the lid on the slow cooker. Cook the chicken for six hours on LOW.

Afterwards, shred the chicken and serve warm.

Blast-Off Barbacoa Chicken

Recipe Makes 6 Servings
Nutritional Breakdown Per Serving: 210 calories,
4 grams net carbohydrates, 5 grams fat, 33 grams
protein
Prep Time: 10 minutes
Cook Time: 4 hours

Ingredients:
2 ½ pounds chicken breasts
8 ounces chipotles in adobo sauce
1 quartered onion
5 garlic cloves
1 tbsp. cumin
1 tsp. oregano
¾ cup chicken broth
salt and pepper to taste

Directions:
Begin by salting and peppering the chicken. Place the chicken, onion, and the garlic cloves in the slow cooker.

To the side, stir together the cumin, oregano, adobo sauce, and the chicken broth. Pour this over the chicken and stir.

Cook the chicken on HIGH for four hours. Afterwards, remove the garlic, chipotle peppers and the onions, and shred the chicken with two forks. Serve the onions alongside the chicken.

Chicken Stuffed Green Peppers

Recipe Makes 4 Servings
Nutritional Breakdown Per Serving: 190 calories, 9 grams net carbohydrates, 5 grams fat, 14 grams protein
Prep Time: 20 minutes
Cook Time: 8 hours

Ingredients:
10 ounces ground chicken
1 diced onion
½ cup diced broccoli
5 ounces diced tomatoes
5 ounces tomato paste
1/3 cup chopped cilantro
4 green peppers
1 tsp. cumin

Directions:
Begin by slicing the tops of the bell peppers off. Remove the seeds from the pepper.

To the side, combine the ground chicken, broccoli, onion, tomatoes, cilantro, and the cumin together. Portion the mixture into the peppers. Top the peppers with their original tops and place them in the slow cooker. Pour a bit of water into the slow cooker so that you cover ½ inch of the bottom of the peppers. Cook the peppers on LOW for eight hours.

Mexican Monday Chicken Quesadillas

Recipe Makes 8 Servings
Nutritional Breakdown Per Serving: 175 calories, 8 grams net carbohydrates, 9 grams fat, 16 grams protein
Prep Time: 15 minutes
Cook Time: 3 hours

Ingredients:
16 ounces boneless and skinless chicken breasts
1 diced onion
1 tsp. garlic powder
1 ½ tsp. oregano
1 diced bell pepper
1 tbsp. oil
1 minced garlic clove
1 ½ cups shredded cheddar cheese
8 low-carbohydrate corn tortillas

Directions:
Begin by slicing the chicken breasts into halves and seasoning the chicken breasts with the various spices. Next, place the corn tortillas in the slow cooker. Top the tortillas with cheese, the sliced chicken, the peppers, and the onions. Add the other tortillas overtop the ingredients.

Place the lid on the slow cooker and allow the ingredients to cook for three hours on HIGH. Take the quesadillas out of the slow cooker and allow them to cool prior to serving.

Parisienne Poulet

Recipe Makes 6 Servings
Nutritional Breakdown Per Serving: 280 calories, 8 grams net carbohydrates, 12 grams fat, 30 grams protein

Ingredients:
6 boneless and skinless chicken breasts
½ cup white wine
11 ounces cream of mushroom soup
1 cup sour cream
5 ounces sliced mushrooms
¼ cup almond flour
salt and pepper to taste

Directions:
Begin by salting and peppering the chicken breasts. Place the chicken breasts in the slow cooker.

To the side in a large bowl, mix together the soup, wine, and the mushrooms. In a different bowl, mix together the almond flour and the sour cream. Stir this sour cream into the wine and mushroom mixture. Pour this over the chicken and cover the slow cooker. Allow the chicken to cook for eight hours on LOW. Enjoy.

Believe in Butter Chicken

Recipe Makes 6 Servings
Nutritional Breakdown Per Serving: 240 calories, 5 grams net carbohydrates, 13 grams fat, 24 grams protein
Prep Time: 15 minutes
Cook Time: 4 hours

Ingredients:
2 pounds diced chicken breasts
1 diced shallot
5 minced garlic cloves
¼ cup yogurt
2 tsp. garam masala
1/3 cup half and half cream
2 ¼ tsp. cayenne pepper
1 tsp. chili powder
2 tbsp. butter
1 tbsp. vegetable oil
1 diced onion
2 tsp. lemon juice
1 minced inch of ginger
1 cup 2% milk
1 cup tomato sauce
salt and pepper to taste

Directions:

Begin by heating the vegetable oil in a skillet. Place the onion and the diced shallot in the oil and heat them, stirring occasionally, for five minutes. Add lemon juice, garam masala, garlic, ginger, chili powder, cumin, and cayenne to the skillet and stir for approximately one minute.

Next, add the tomato sauce and continue to stir for three minutes.

Pour in the yogurt, milk, and the half and half cream. Reduce the heat and allow it to simmer for ten minutes. Pour this mixture into a blender or a food processor and blend until completely combined.

Place the cubed chicken in the slow cooker. Pour the prepared mixture over the chicken, and place the lid on the slow cooker. Allow the chicken to cook on HIGH for four hours. Enjoy.

Rotisserie-Style Chicken

Recipe Makes 10 Servings
**Nutritional Breakdown Per Serving: 180 calories,
2 grams net carbohydrates, 8 grams fat, 17 grams
protein**
Prep Time: 20 minutes
Cook Time: 8 hours

Ingredients:
1- 3 pound chicken with fat removed
1 tsp. salt
1 tsp. garlic powder
½ tsp. basil
1 tsp. smoked paprika
1 lemon
1 tsp. oregano

Directions:
Begin by forming five balls from aluminum foil. Place
these at the very bottom of the slow cooker.

To the side, mix together the spices and the juice you
squeeze from the lemon. Rub this spice mixture over
the entire chicken.

Push the lemon into the cavity of the chicken and
place the chicken over the aluminum.

Place the lid on the slow cooker and allow it to cook for a full eight hours.

Southern Living Chicken Lettuce Wraps

Recipe Makes 6 Servings
Nutritional Breakdown Per Serving: 145 calories, 5 grams net carbohydrates, 0 grams fat, 24 grams protein
Prep Time: 10 minutes
Cook Time: 4 hours

Ingredients:
1 ½ pounds skinless and boneless chicken breasts
1 diced celery stalk
1 diced onion
3 minced garlic cloves
14 ounces chicken broth
½ cup buffalo sauce
6 large Iceberg lettuce leaves
1 ½ cups shredded carrots

Directions:

Begin by bringing the onion, celery stalk, chicken, broth, and garlic together in the slow cooker. Cover the slow cooker and allow it to cook for four hours on HIGH.

Next, place the chicken on a side plate. Keep half a cup of the chicken broth and toss out the rest. Shred up the chicken with two forks and place it back in the slow cooker with the remaining broth. Pour in the buffalo sauce and allow the chicken to cook for an additional half hour.

Portion out the chicken into the lettuce leaves and add the carrots overtop. Wrap the lettuce into "wraps" and enjoy.

Moroccan Chicken Marrakesh

Recipe Makes 8 Servings
Nutritional Breakdown Per Serving: 230 calories,
9.9 grams net carbohydrates, 7 grams fat, 18
grams protein
Prep Time: 10 minutes
Cook Time: 5 hours

Ingredients:
1 diced onion
2 diced sweet potatoes
2 diced carrots
3 minced garlic cloves
1 ½ tsp. ground turmeric
1 tsp. cumin
15 ounces chickpeas
2 tsp. parsley
1 tsp. cinnamon
14 ounces diced tomatoes
salt and pepper to taste

Directions:
Begin by preparing the vegetables and pour together the chickpeas, sweet potatoes, carrots, garlic, onion, and the chicken breasts in the slow cooker.

To the side, mix together turmeric, cinnamon, cumin, salt, pepper, and parsley. Stir well. Pour the tomatoes into this mixture and continue to stir. Pour this mixture over the chicken breasts, and cover the slow cooker. Cook for five hours on HIGH.

Rosemary Rub Chicken

Recipe Makes 8 Servings
Nutritional Breakdown Per Serving: 205 calories, 1 grams net carbohydrates, 13 grams fat, 18 grams protein
Prep Time: 10 minutes
Cook Time: 8 hours

Ingredients:
2 pounds skinless and boneless chicken breasts
½ cup butter
¾ cup chicken broth
6 minced garlic cloves
1 tbsp. rosemary

Directions:
Begin by bringing the garlic and butter together in a skillet. Cook the garlic for about five minutes. Pour

this mixture into the slow cooker, and roll the chicken breasts around in the butter. Sprinkle the rosemary over the chicken, and salt and pepper it. Pour the broth into the slow cooker and cover it. Cook the chicken for eight hours on LOW.

Lemon and Garlic Chicken

Recipe Makes 6 Servings
Nutritional Breakdown Per Serving: 190 calories,
1 gram net carbohydrates, 7 grams fat, 29 grams
protein
Prep Time: 15 minutes
Cook Time: 6 hours

Ingredients:
½ cup water
1 tsp. oregano
2 pounds boneless and skinless chicken breasts
2 tbsp. butter
juice from 1 lemon
1 tsp. chicken bouillon
3 minced garlic cloves
1 tsp. chopped parsley
1 tsp. salt
1 tsp. pepper

Directions:
Begin by mixing together the oregano with the salt and the pepper. Rub this spice mixture over the chicken. To the side, place the butter in a skillet and allow the butter to melt. Place the chicken in the butter and allow it to brown for five minutes. Next, place the chicken in the slow cooker.

In this skillet, place the garlic, lemon juice, water, and the bouillon together and stir. Allow this mixture to boil, and pour it over the chicken.

Cover the slow cooker and cook the chicken on LOW for six hours. Place the parsley in the slow cooker and allow it to cook for an additional fifteen minutes. Serve the chicken and enjoy.

Cowboy Carefree Chicken

Recipe Makes 6 Servings
Nutritional Breakdown Per Serving: 170 calories,
8 grams net carbohydrates, 2 grams fat, 28 grams
protein
Prep Time: 5 minutes
Cook time: 6 hours

Ingredients:
6 halved chicken breasts
2 cups salsa
2 tbsp. brown sugar
1 tbsp. Dijon mustard

Directions:
Begin by placing the chicken in the slow cooker. To the side, mix together the salsa, brown sugar, and the mustard. Stir well, and pour this mixture over the chicken.

Cook the chicken for six hours on LOW, and serve with vegetables.

Catchy Chicken Cacciatore

Recipe Makes 6 Servings
Nutritional Breakdown Per Serving: 230 calories,
9 grams net carbohydrates, 6 grams fat, 28 grams
protein
Prep Time: 10 minutes
Cook Time: 7 hours

Ingredients:
2 pounds skinless and boneless chicken breasts
1 diced onion
5 tbsp. tomato paste
14 ounces diced tomatoes
1 diced bell pepper
5 minced garlic cloves
1 tbsp. oregano
½ cup red wine
1 pound diced mushrooms

1 tsp. red pepper flakes

Directions:

Place everything except the chicken in the slow cooker. Stir the ingredients together and then add the chicken. Stir well in order to coat it. Place the cover on the slow cooker and cook on LOW for six hours. Enjoy!

Savoury Chicken Stroganoff

Recipe Makes 4 Servings
Nutritional Breakdown Per Serving: 450 calories, 9 grams net carbohydrates, 31 grams fat, 33 grams protein
Prep Time: 10 minutes
Cook Time: 6 hours

Ingredients:
4 boneless and skinless chicken breasts
¼ cup butter
8 ounces cream cheese
10 ounces cream of chicken soup
1 ½ tsp. Italian seasoning

Directions:
Begin by placing the chicken, butter, and the Italian seasoning together in the slow cooker. Stir well and cook the chicken on LOW for six hours.

Next, add the soup and the cream cheese to the mixture. Stir well, and cook on HIGH for an additional thirty minutes. Serve warm.

Lime Cilantro Chicken

Recipe Makes 6 Servings
Nutritional Breakdown Per Serving: 270 calories, 8 grams net carbohydrates, 4 grams fat, 45 grams protein
Prep Time: 5 minutes
Cook Time: 8 hours

Ingredients:
16 ounces salsa of your choice
juice from 2 limes
1 package taco seasoning
3 tbsp. cilantro
2 ½ pounds boneless and skinless chicken breasts

Directions:
Pour the salsa, lime juice, taco seasoning, and the cilantro together into the slow cooker. Stir well. Place

the chicken in the slow cooker and stir in order to coat the chicken. Cover the slow cooker and cook on LOW for eight hours. Afterwards, shred the chicken with forks and enjoy.

Ginger Teriyaki Chicken

Recipe Makes 4 Servings
Nutritional Breakdown Per Serving: 140 calories,
1 gram net carbohydrates, 1 gram fat, 28 grams
protein
Prep Time: 10 minutes
 Cook Time: 6 hours

Ingredients:
1/3 cup water
¼ cup white wine
½ tsp. ginger
3 minced garlic cloves
¼ cup soy sauce
4 skinless and boneless chicken breasts

Directions:

Begin by mixing together the white wine, garlic cloves, water, soy sauce, and ginger. Stir well, and pour the mixture into a baggy. Place the chicken in the baggy, as well, and pulse the bag around in order to completely coat the chicken. Afterwards, place the chicken in the slow cooker and allow it to cook for six hours on LOW.

Low-Carb Chicken Enchiladas

Recipe Makes 12 Servings
Nutritional Breakdown Per Serving: 180 calories,
4 grams net carbohydrates, 11 grams fat, 18
grams protein
Prep Time: 5 minutes
Cook Time: 8 hours

Ingredients:
10 ounces cream of chicken soup
3 cups sour cream
2 ½ pounds boneless and skinless chicken breasts
5 ounces diced green chilies
2 tbsp. onion powder

Directions:
Begin by pouring the sour cream, soup, onion powder, and the chilies together in the slow cooker. Stir well.

Next, place the chicken in the slow cooker and completely cover it with the creamy mixture. Cover the slow cooker and allow the chicken to cook for 8 hours on LOW. Serve this mixture over cauliflower rice.

Asian-Inspired BBQ Chicken

Recipe Makes 8 Servings
Nutritional Breakdown Per Serving: 315 calories, 10 grams net carbohydrates, 20 grams fat, 20 grams protein
Prep Time: 5 minutes
Cook Time: 8 hours

Ingredients:
1/3 cup soy sauce
2 tbsp. olive oil
3 tbsp. lime juice
¼ cup brown sugar
2 tsp. ginger
4 minced garlic cloves
1 tsp. garam masala
½ tsp. sesame oil
8 boneless and skinless chicken breasts
2 diced onions

Directions:
Begin by preparing the onions. Pour the different oils and soy sauces into the slow cooker. Add the brown sugar and stir well. After you've gathered everything except for the lime juice into the slow cooker, add the chicken breasts. Coat the chicken breasts with the sauce on the inside of the slow cooker, and place the lid on top. Cook the dinner on LOW for eight hours.

Afterwards, pour the lime juice over the chicken and serve warm.

Roasted Paprika Chicken

Recipe Makes 6 Servings
Nutritional Breakdown Per Serving: 300 calories, 6 grams net carbohydrates, 9 grams fat, 45 grams protein
Prep Time: 5 minutes
Cook Time: 8 hours

Ingredients:
2 tbsp. olive oil
2 tbsp. paprika
1 tsp. cinnamon
1 tsp. cayenne
3 ½ pound chicken
1 diced onion

Directions:
Begin by slicing up the chicken into different "serving" sizes. To the side, mix together the olive oil and the spices. Rub this spice mixture over the chicken and place the chicken in the slow cooker. Place the onion around the chicken and place the lid on the slow cooker. Allow the chicken to cook on LOW for eight hours. Enjoy.

Conclusion

"Chicken Slow Cooker Cookbook" fuels you through those hectic fall and winter months with delicious and dynamic soups, stews, chilies, and dinner recipes. Bring together the proper spices, sauces, and stunning garlic flavours and leave the recipes to assemble themselves as you go about with your business. Come home to a dinner rich with nutrients, with muscle-building protein, and with heart healthy components.

Fight back against cancer and rid yourself of sadness and depression with the serotonin boost. Bring essential health into your life, and allow the low carbohydrate, 10 grams-or-less nature of each recipe to help you drop weight and feel more like your true self. You can create a lively, nutritive diet plan that suits your jam-packed lifestyle, and you can build essential, flavorful recipes without a single ounce of cooking know-how. Allow this recipe book to guide you on your path to health and joyful eating.

51272591R00051

Made in the USA
Lexington, KY
24 April 2016